Spiritual Warfare in Mission

MARY ANNE VOELKEL
AND JACK VOELKEL

Series editors:
Nikki A. Toyama-Szeto and Tom Lin

IVP Books

An imprint of InterVarsity Press
Downers Grove, Illinois

InterVarsity Press
P.O. Box 1400, Downers Grove, IL 60515-1426
World Wide Web: www.ivpress.com
E-mail: email@ivpress.com

*InterVarsity Press® is the book-publishing division of InterVarsity Christian Fellowship/USA®, a
movement of students and faculty active on campus at hundreds of universities, colleges and schools
of nursing in the United States of America, and a member movement of the International Fellowship of
Evangelical Students. For information about local and regional activities, write Public Relations Dept.,
InterVarsity Christian Fellowship/USA, 6400 Schroeder Rd., P.O. Box 7895, Madison, WI 53707-7895, or
visit the IVCF website at <www.intervarsity.org>.*

*All Scripture quotations, unless otherwise indicated, are taken from the Holy Bible, Today's New
International Version®, NIV® Copyright © 1973, 1978, 1984, 2011 by Biblica, Inc.™ Used by permission.
All rights reserved worldwide.*

*While all stories in this book are true, some names and identifying information in this book have been
changed to protect the privacy of the individuals involved.*

Cover design: Cindy Kiple
Images: abstract background: © Matthew Hertel/iStockphoto
    Lightning bolt: © Matthew Hertel/iStockphoto
ISBN 978-0-8308-3464-8

Printed in the United States of America ∞

Library of Congress Cataloging-in-Publication Data has been requested.

P 21 20 19 18 17 16 15 14 13 12 11 10 9 8 7 6 5 4 3 2 1
Y 30 29 28 27 26 25 24 23 22 21 20 19 18 17 16 15 14 13 12

To our three children—Alan, Jon and Lisa

Contents

I have given you authority . . . to overcome all the power of the enemy. . . . However, do not rejoice that the spirits submit to you, but rejoice that your names are written in heaven. (Luke 10:19-20)

The crowd kept waiting, but nothing happened. An endless minute went by, and then another. Canadian evangelist T. V. Thomas stood at the podium trying to begin his talk about a controversial subject: *Is Jesus Christ the Only Way to Find God?*

It was the 1996 Urbana Student Missions Conference and 19,621 delegates waited expectantly. Try as he might, T. V. could not say a single word. He couldn't have been hoarse, for the intercession team had prayed with him only minutes before. Yet here he was, speechlessly clutching his throat and growing increasingly agitated. Something invisible seemed to be choking him.

Urbana director Dan Harrison rushed forward to offer water. But many in the audience sensed that the problem was spiritual, not physical, and they cried out, "Pray! Pray!"

As Dan Harrison prayed for the speaker, Mary Anne, leader of the Intercession Team, sensed she was to stand inconspicuously behind the platform and raise her arms in worship and prayer. Two intercessors slipped outside the Assembly Hall to ask God for protection and in the name of Jesus command the evil spirit that was choking T. V. to release his throat. Gradually, his voice returned. The longer we prayed the stronger and more powerful his words became. When he finished, the delegates exploded in a roar of applause not so much for T. V. but for the Lord himself, who had delivered his servant from a direct attack by the enemy.

The delegates learned more than the uniqueness of Christ that day. They lived and breathed spiritual warfare in the context of mission.

WHAT IS SPIRITUAL WARFARE?

Before reading on, stop for a moment and think: What do you know about spiritual warfare? Have you ever experienced it?

We did a little survey to discover what some Christians in the United States and Canada think about the subject. We discovered that most don't think much about it at all. A contemporary student worker writes:

> The reality of evil and its influence on daily life is fairly unfamiliar territory to those I work with. It's a totally new idea that some kind of dynamic systemic evil could energize interpersonal conflict or temptations. A few may pray for protection now and then but most don't even feel a need to do that.[1]

The concepts we Christians *do* hold regarding spiritual warfare vary greatly, depending on our backgrounds and knowledge of Scripture. New believers may have a vague idea of evil, but it's often shaped by fantasy movies (witches, vampires, avatars), television, fiction or social media.

Christians involved in Bible study usually have a deeper appreciation of prayer and the power and authority of Jesus, along with some understanding of spiritual warfare. Many, however, say that they have little personal experience in these areas, nor do they know how to apply the authority of Jesus over evil to their own lives, intercession or outreach.

This booklet offers a brief biblical perspective on spiritual warfare in the context of mission. It includes Scripture, practical suggestions and stories to illustrate each point, plus resources in the bibliography for further investigation. We give special thanks to our colleagues in the Colombian IFES movement,[2] Unidad Cristiana Universitaria (UCU), as well as to our prayer partners in InterVarsity Christian Fellowship/USA and InterVarsity Christian Fellowship of Canada. So much of what we have learned grew out of our rich fellowship with them.

Paul's understanding of spiritual warfare. The apostle Paul often used the metaphor of spiritual warfare to help young Christians overcome the struggles they were facing. The fledgling church at Corinth, for instance, was riddled with moral failure, reeling from divisions and in danger of exchanging their solid foundation of faith for the lies of false apostles (2 Corinthians 11:2-4).

To help them, Paul wrote:

> For though we live in the world, we do not wage war as the world does. The weapons we fight with are not the weapons of the world. On the contrary, they have divine power to demolish strongholds. We demolish arguments and every pretension that sets itself up against the knowledge of God, and we take captive every thought to make it obedient to Christ. (2 Corinthians 10:3-5)

Although Paul uses military terms "wage war" and "weapons we fight with," he is quick to distance this type of conflict from any kind of physical violence. The weapons he suggests throughout all his epistles are spiritual and come from God, not ourselves. In 2 Corinthians 10:3-5, Paul uses the weapon of truth to "demolish strongholds" in the minds of the Corinthians. English expositor Derek Prince underscores the importance of this mental battlefield:

> We absolutely must understand the battleground is in the realm of the mind. Satan is waging an all-out war to captivate the minds of the human race. He is building . . . fortresses in their minds and it is our responsibility as God's representatives to use our spiritual weapons to break down these strongholds . . . and bring men and women . . . to the obedience of Christ. What a staggering assignment that is![3]

Our first encounter with such mental and spiritual strongholds took place in Bogotá, Colombia, where we served with the Latin America Mission, helping to pioneer a student ministry. We moved in across the street from the National University and discovered that the prevailing ideology on campus was Marxism, replete with frequent, strident anti-American demonstrations. How could we become a part of such a university?

Jack applied for a teaching position, but there were no vacancies. We prayer walked the campus each night, Joshua-style, and asked God for an opening. After seven days of prayer, the English department phoned. A colleague had resigned, and they offered his position to Jack. With great joy, he became an English professor and Mary Anne enrolled as a part-time student in social work. Both of us began befriending students.

Tremendous mental and spiritual barriers, however, stood between the gospel and the first Colombians who accepted our invitation to Bible study lunches. As Americans we were considered exploitative capitalists and probable members of the CIA. We were *evangélicos* (Protestants), often considered a false sect in this Roman Catholic culture, and we followed a Jesus they could not yet comprehend.

To bring down these strongholds we would need all the love, wisdom and spiritual weapons that the Lord could offer us.

Paul's conversion and call gave us clues about how to go forward. As a zealous Jewish Pharisee, he held strong mental and religious objections to Jews who believed that Jesus was divine. As he traveled to Damascus to imprison Christians, Paul met the living Christ, personally! His worldview crashed, and amid the broken pieces Jesus spoke to him and gave him a new vision and reason for living: "I am sending you to [Jews and Gentiles] to open their eyes and turn them from darkness to light, and from the power of Satan to God, so that they may receive forgiveness of sins and a place among those who are sanctified by faith in me" (Acts 26:17-18).

In this verse we discover that spiritual warfare *begins with God* and not the enemy. God is on a mission to rescue prisoners from "darkness" and the "power of Satan," and bring them into the kingdom of his beloved Son. He invites us who believe in Jesus to join him. We could see that our modest attempts to reach students for Jesus on a spiritually hostile campus *was* spiritual warfare. We were invading enemy territory, and God was using his Word to bring students to himself.

Very soon the enemy launched a counterattack. It happened on a Friday night at large group meeting. Someone invited Amelia, a new believer, to join our fellowship. Her father, Alvaro, however, was very suspicious. As a Colombian police officer, he was convinced that we were dealing drugs, so he decided to accompany his daughter, feigning interest in the meeting. No one realized that he had a squad car circling our block waiting for his signal so they could rush in to make the sting.

The Lord in his mercy protected us. He used the teaching that night to demolish the strongholds in Alvaro's mind. Alvaro forgot about the squad car as he sat enthralled by the gospel. In the months that followed, all of Amelia's family became committed Christians. Over the years Amelia has led scores of people to Jesus.

Spiritual warfare defined. Spiritual warfare, then, in its simplest form is our partnership with God as he advances his kingdom behind enemy lines. Satan and his forces often counterattack, seeking to thwart us and our inroads with every scheme, wile or fiery dart they can muster (Ephesians 6:10-20). In the face of their attacks, we as Christians are to wage both a defensive and offensive spiritual battle:

- *Defensive.* We "put on the full armor of God" to protect ourselves from the schemes of Satan. Satan is evil, mean and nasty, absolutely committed to the destruction of individuals and nations. But we don't stop there. Jesus isn't a bomb shelter to protect the chosen.

- *Offensive.* Jesus calls us to partner with him in rescuing men and women from darkness and in extending his kingdom. He offers us powerful and effective resources. Some of these include:

  » a growing, dependent relationship with our triune God

  » worship and intercession in the context of community

  » costly, loving service and bold, thoughtful evangelism

  » healing and deliverance

WHO IS OUR ENEMY?

When talking about Satan and the demons under Satan's control, C. S. Lewis warned of two extremes:

> There are two equal and opposite errors into which our race can fall about the devils. One is to disbelieve in their existence. The other is to believe, and to feel an excessive and unhealthy interest in them. They themselves are equally pleased by both errors and hail a materialist or a magician with the same delight.[4]

The Scriptures dispel any doubts we may have about the reality of Satan. He was present in the garden of Eden (Genesis 3), tempted Jesus at the onset of his ministry (Matthew 4:1-11) and is mentioned more than fifty times in the New Testament.

Where did Satan come from? While there are no precise references to Satan's origin, two prophetic passages describing pagan kings seem to refer to Satan as well. He was apparently a high-ranking angel called Lucifer, or Star of the Morning, "full of wisdom and perfect in beauty" (Isaiah 14:12; Ezekiel 28:12-17). According to Isaiah his heart became proud, and seeking to make himself "like the Most High," he rebelled and fell into sin (Isaiah 14:13-14, 19). But Lucifer didn't fall alone.

Angels serving under Lucifer's dominion apparently rebelled with him and became a hierarchy of evil spirits under his authority. Paul describes these evil beings in Ephesians 6:12: "Our struggle is not against flesh and blood, but against the rulers, against the authorities, against the powers of this dark world and against the spiritual forces of evil in the heavenly realms."

The Bible uses several names to describe Satan and his character. Jesus calls him "the prince of this world" (John 12:31; 14:30; 16:11), a "murderer" and "the father of lies" (John 8:44). The word *Satan* means "adversary," the one who "accuses [us] before our God day and night" (Revelation 12:10). Satan is commonly called the "devil," which literally means "deceiver."

Satan's deceitfulness was evident from the beginning. Although our loving Creator lavishly offered the first man and woman every resource on earth, except the fruit from a single tree, Satan approached Eve to cast doubts about God's generosity and goodness. "Did God really say, 'You must not eat from *any* tree in the garden'?" he slyly asked (Genesis 3:1, emphasis added).

In the dialogue that followed, the enemy enticed Eve to sin by the same three-step process he so often uses with us:

1. First he tempted Eve to *doubt* God and his word ("Did God really say . . . ?" [Genesis 3:1]).

2. Then he tempted her to *disbelieve* God ("You will not certainly die!" [Genesis 3:4]).

3.   Finally, Eve and Adam chose to *disobey* God [Genesis 3:6-7]).

Their disobedience brought instantaneous spiritual death. Their physical death would follow. Theologians call this tragic betrayal the "Fall."

What was Satan really up to? We as human beings are God's beloved, created in his image to know and worship him. He gave our forefathers free will and some of his own authority to govern the whole earth. Satan hungered for both worship and power. He knew that Adam and Eve's authority depended on their living in fellowship with God and under his sovereignty. If he could only get them to disobey the *one* commandment that demonstrated their submission to the Lord, he would gain what he most desired: authority over the human race and control over the world they had been created to rule (Romans 6:16).

The results of the Fall. We will categorize the catastrophic consequences of the Fall under three familiar headings: the *world*, the *flesh* and the *devil*. As we take a brief look at each one, think about how they interplay in the spiritual warfare you face in your own context.

The world. New Testament professor Clinton Arnold defines the world as

> The unhealthy social environments in which we live—[including] the ungodly aspects of culture, peer pressure, values, traditions, "what is in," "what is uncool," customs, philosophies, and attitudes—prevailing worldview assumptions of the day that stand contrary to the biblical understanding of reality and . . . values.[5]

The manifestations of *the world* obviously vary from culture to culture, but the *world system* at its core is contrary to God's revealed truth and stands in opposition to his kingdom. InterVarsity regional director for New York and New Jersey, Jason Gaboury, gives this penetrating analysis about how it plays out among secular young adults today:

> Non-Christian students are spiritually curious, but increasingly many lack a concept of sin. They fear that moral absolutes [are] somehow evil and resent the idea that God may have moral requirements. This turns them in on themselves in ways that are deeply dehumanizing.
> Refusing to accept any moral standard, except what they choose

or feel, students deceive themselves into thinking that they are good despite the fact that they cheat, lie, slander, steal, dishonor their parents and engage in addictive and destructive sexual practices. As a result I am constantly praying John 16:8 in evangelistic situations, that the Holy Spirit would convict of sin, of the righteousness of Christ, and of the reality of judgment.[6]

The flesh. Although we were created in the majestically beautiful image of God, through the Fall our nature became imprisoned in self-centeredness and sin. "The acts of the flesh are obvious," writes the apostle Paul, "sexual immorality, impurity, . . . hatred, discord, jealousy, . . . selfish ambition, . . . and the like" (Galatians 5:19-21), and "those who are in the realm of the flesh cannot please God" (Romans 8:5-8).

God in his grace did not allow our sin to blot out all aspects of his image. We still have the capacity to think, create, pursue scientific knowledge, harness the forces of nature and, to a greater or lesser extent, care for one another. However, as P. E. Hughes writes,

> The efforts of fallen human beings are cursed with frustration. . . . History shows that the very discoveries and advances which have promised most good to mankind have through misuse brought great evils in their train. The individual who does not love God does not love his fellow men. He is driven by selfish motives.[7]

The devil. When humans chose to listen to Satan and not to God, they submitted to Satan's authority. Unregenerate humans are under his dominion whether they know it or not. "The whole world is under the control of the evil one," observes the apostle John (1 John 5:19). Satan blinds the minds of unbelievers "so that they cannot see the light of the gospel that displays the glory of Christ, who is the image of God" (2 Corinthians 4:4). The devil's chief aim is to keep individuals from coming to know Jesus as Savior and Lord.

Satan works more overtly among persons or groups who actively seek his power, like those practicing the occult, witchcraft, voodoo, Wicca, spiritism or Satanism. He works more covertly in cultures like ours that highly value the intellectual, the scientific and the material rather than a worldview that includes spiritual reality. He still ensnares people in our Western cultures, however, through lies, unbelief, pride, materialism, greed, injustice, racism, pornography, sexual sin, moral decadence and so much more.

It is important to note that Satan is *not divine*. Only our triune God is God. Spiritual warfare is *not* a dualistic battle between equals. Rather, our sovereign Lord empowers his church to co-labor with him as he advances the kingdom in a world deceived and enslaved by Satan.

Does Satan attack Christians today? The following are just a few recent examples

- Cindy sleeps with the lights on, because she fears her nightmares and senses an evil presence in her room.

- A student group in Canada passionately shares Jesus, but recently suffered intense opposition through car accidents, sickness, break-ins, computer crashes, temptations and discouragement.

- Kevin, a dedicated missionary, is secretly in bondage to Internet pornography.

- The students and staff on an East Coast campus feel intimidated and harassed by "the powers that be."

- Carla, an abuse victim, struggles with shame and rejection and *cannot* believe that God really loves her.

As you read this list, can you relate? Can you add examples of your own? If any of those cases describe you or your friends, would you know what to do about the problem or where to turn for help? We didn't!

We received a wake-up call when Francis MacNutt came to talk to our students about knowing Christ personally and experiencing his healing power. In the middle of MacNutt's talk, a grad student we had never seen before began to act very strangely and then screamed. We were as shocked as our students and hadn't a clue about what to do.

Francis recognized immediately that the man was demonized. We took him to another room for privacy, where the student told us how he had opened himself to the enemy. Francis led him in prayer to confess and renounce sin and Satan, and then bound the demon in Jesus' name and commanded it to leave. After a struggle, it did.

A FRESH LOOK AT JESUS

Although Jack was the son and grandson of missionaries to Korea and had known Jesus since childhood, and although he had gone to seminary and planted a church in Canada, he had never encountered a demonized person before; nor had Mary Anne.

The whole experience was like a page out of the Gospels. We both realized we needed to take a fresh look at Jesus and learn how to minister in his power and authority. Few of us grasp a fraction of the magnitude of what Jesus actually accomplished on the cross:

- He *destroyed* the work of the devil. (1 John 3:8)

- He *disarmed* the powers and authorities. (Colossians 2:15)

- He *overcame* death and brought life. (Romans 6:23)

- He *took* our judgment and brought reconciliation. (2 Corinthians 5:19)

- He *became* our sin and *made us* righteous. (2 Corinthians 5:21)

- He *crucifies* the power of the flesh; now we can obey God. (Romans 8:10)

Most importantly, Jesus won back *all the authority* the enemy stole from humans as a result of the Fall. After his resurrection his last words to his followers were, "All authority in heaven and on earth has been given to me. Therefore, go and make disciples of all nations" (Matthew 28:18-19).

Jesus now sits at God's right hand, "far above all rule and authority, power and dominion" (Ephesians 1:21). In his name and authority we can stand against the wiles of the devil and *resist him,* firm in the faith (James 4:7; 1 Peter 5:9).

Although Satan is a defeated foe, he has authority and power over those who are not yet part God's kingdom. He will stay here on earth while the Lord works through believers to turn people "from darkness to light, and from the power of Satan to God" (Acts 26:18). If God were to judge Satan right now, all who are under his dominion would be judged as well. Peter reminds us that God is patient, not wanting any to perish, but all to be saved (2 Peter 3:9, 15). At the end of time, Satan and his minions will be judged and Christ's victory over the darkness will be complete.

PREPARING TO ADVANCE THE KINGDOM

"Spiritual warfare does not begin with a clash of weapons, but with strengthening our relationship with God," says Mary Ellen Conners.[8]

Fuller Seminary professor emeritus Charles Kraft notes that the secret of Jesus' power and authority on earth came from his intimacy with the Father and his submission to him. Our power and authority come from the same sources.

> In the New Testament, both power and authority flow from the work of Christ. . . . Jesus received power from the Holy Spirit . . . and his authority [came] from maintaining his intimacy with the Father. At the end of his ministry on earth . . . he gave his followers the Holy Spirit, the source of his power, and advised them to keep close to him.[9]

Jesus did not do miracles, live a holy life and overcome the enemy because he was God. He did so because he depended on the Father and the power of his Spirit for everything he did and said (John 4:24; 5:19, 20, 30; 6:38; 6:57). So can we.

Starting the day with our triune God. We find it helpful to begin each morning, no matter how busy the day, with thanksgiving and praise (music, a psalm or our own prayers). Worship lifts our spirits and banishes any heaviness of heart. Listening to God's voice in Scripture keeps us connected with him and guides our prayers and daily life. Expressing our love to him and then receiving his *unconditional love for us* deepens intimacy and feeds our souls (Ephesians 3:14-21).

The armor of God. Paul clarifies the locus of our spiritual battle: we are not struggling against "flesh and blood, but against . . . the spiritual forces of evil in the heavenly realms" (Ephesians 6:12).

For this reason he insists that we must strengthen ourselves "in the Lord and in his mighty power" (Ephesians 6:10) and "put on the full armor of God" (Ephesians 6:11). Mike Flynn, pastor and trainer of prayer ministers, notes that he and his family were under constant harassment from the enemy until he began to literally pray Ephesians 6:10-20 over himself and his family *every day.* The oppression then quickly lifted.[10]

One way to "put on the full armor of God" is to turn Ephesians 6:10-18 into prayer:

- Ask Jesus to make you strong in the Lord and in his mighty power (v. 10).
- Pray that he would teach you his truth and that you would believe it (v. 14).
- Ask Jesus to cleanse you and give you his righteousness (v. 14; 2 Corinthians 5:21).
- Ask Jesus to prepare you to share the gospel with others and pray for your non-Christian friends (v. 15).
- Ask Jesus to protect you and resist in his name any "flaming arrows" that come your way, such as fear, doubt, lies, temptations or discouragements (v. 16).
- Ask God to cleanse and protect your mind and remove unhelpful thoughts or images you've received from movies, books or the Internet (v. 17).
- Pray the Scripture you are reading for yourself and others (vv. 17-18).
- Ask the Holy Spirit to fill and empower you, guide your prayers and lead you all day long (v. 18).

OVERCOMING THE COUNTERATTACKS OF THE ENEMY

Once we have communed with Jesus and are clothed with his armor, we are ready to live our day in him. Along the way we will face challenges and difficulties. "In this world," warns Jesus, "you will have trouble. But take heart! I have overcome the world" (John 16:33).

Most of the problems we face are *not* demonic. They arise from the stresses of everyday life in the context of a fallen world and our sinful flesh. We need discernment from the Holy Spirit to assess the sources of our problems and what he would have us do about them. However, the enemy *does* seem to exacerbate the problems we have. He preys on our brokenness, "piles on" condemnation and discouragement, and tempts us to doubt, disobey or depend on ourselves.

The attacks from within. Because of our fallen natures and broken families the enemy has built-in ways to attack us. He can aim his arrows at our minds, bodies, wills, emotions or memories. In this section we will look at five of these vulnerable places *within* us.

Overcoming assaults on our identity. Many of us come from dysfunctional families and often didn't receive enough love, acceptance or affirmation to establish a secure identity. Physical, emotional or sexual abuse greatly compound this problem. If the enemy can imprison us in guilt, fear, shame or rejection, he can keep us from believing that God (or anyone else) unconditionally loves us.

The pain in our hearts is almost always wrapped around lies we believe about ourselves. We can ask Jesus to clarify lies we believe and tell us the truth so that we may be healed. It is important to bring our wounds to Jesus and find his healing through forgiving those who hurt us. Receiving prayer ministry or counseling and reading books on inner healing can be extremely helpful. It is *essential* to become a part of a loving, healing community. Isolation deepens despair.

Overcoming sin. As we continued our student ministry in Colombia, God raised up a wonderful group of students and staff. Worship soared and the presence of God in the prayer meetings made them the most popular gatherings of the week. The loving community that emerged set such a high bar for genuine fellowship that few of us have experienced anything like it since.

But then came the dry times. And they came more than once. Invisible issues seemed to erode our fellowship and the sense of God's presence. As prayer and worship became routine, outreach waned. Some students grew for a while and then plateaued or stopped coming. Conflicts took root in the deep unhealed brokenness of our hearts, and we couldn't fix them.

Was this an attack of the enemy? Did we need to pray more? Were we doing something wrong?

We longed for refreshment and searched the Scripture. Acts 3:19 confronted us: "Repent, then, and turn to God, so that your sins may be wiped out, and times of refreshing may come from the Lord." We had allowed *sin* into our lives and relationships, and this made us vulnerable to enemy attack. We set aside Saturday mornings for prayer and fasting. We confessed our sin individually and as a group. Responding to God's Word with obedience brought renewal.

Overcoming bondage. As the years passed, our student group became a movement that spread to other cities and then countries. One day, Jack was teaching a group in Medellín, Colombia. A new convert confessed with great anxiety, "I feel like I have two forces fighting within me." When Jack asked him about his past, he mentioned that both his parents had been deeply involved in the occult and had officially dedicated him to Satan. The young man forgave his parents, confessed the sins involved in his dedication, and renounced it and Satan as well. As Jack began to pray for him, he shook violently. Jack bound the evil spirit within him and after a prolonged struggle it left.

We call this kind of bondage "demonization" or demonic oppression.[11] The demon becomes attached to some area of a person's life. Demonization is a common occurrence in the Gospels, and casting out demons or "unclean spirits" was a significant part of Jesus' ministry.

People often ask us if a Christian can be demonized. Pastor and author Tom White gives this helpful answer:

> The believer . . . may need deliverance from spirits that afflict either from an outward source or from an inward attachment. . . . Typically, such spirits gain their influence through pre-conversion sin. They are tenacious and must be exposed and expelled. The Christian can thus be "demonized" (Greek: "have a spirit"), but not "possessed." Possession connotes a totality of ownership and control incompatible with the eternal ownership of a soul by God.[12]

He adds, "Scripture does not exclude the possibility [that a Christian may have a demon resident within him or her], and clinical reality affirms it time and time again."[13]

Some of the doorways through which evil spirits may enter include participation in the occult, victimization (through incest, rape, abuse, occult rituals), persistent sin and moral compromise, or deep roots of rejection, resentment or rebellion. It is instructive to note that the church fathers included casting out evil spirits in their classes for new Christians. They expected that pagans coming out of idolatry would naturally be demonized.[14] Tom White explains how the early church took care of this issue.

> After a precise confession of their pre-Christian sins, [the new believers] renounced all allegiance to Satan and formally closed the doors to his continued influence. [They also] renounced their allegiances to the gods and goddesses, [while] the Christian leaders working with them [laid] their hands on them and commanded the foul spirits to depart.[15]

We might do well in today's world to do the same thing.

If you struggle with oppression or bondage, or know someone who does, we encourage you to seek help. We recommend the books in the bibliography, including Neil Anderson's *Steps to Freedom in Christ*.[16] Anderson encourages readers to list, confess and renounce all occult practices, to forgive those who have hurt us, and to ask forgiveness for all known sin.

Overcoming bitterness and relational sin. A Christian leader recently sent us this urgent prayer request: "Aggravated interpersonal conflict does seem to be a strategy of the world, flesh, and the devil to undermine the work of mission. Please pray God's mercy in the days ahead as we face a rash of relational crises."[17]

The enemy seeks to disenchant, divide and destroy. He gains a foothold in our lives and fellowships through unresolved anger and conflicts. "In your anger," advises Paul, "do not sin. Do not let the sun go down while you are still angry, and do not give the devil a foothold" (Ephesians 4:26-27).

The word *foothold* in Greek means "a spatial geographic place of influence and control."[18] The devil knows that unresolved anger turns into resentment and can cause "a bitter root [to grow up] to cause trouble and defile many" (Hebrews 12:15).

We learned the importance of not giving a foothold to the devil in the second week of our marriage when a conflict resulted in anger, silence and tears. As we faced that first painful misunderstanding, God somehow led us to Ephesians 4:26-27. We made a lifetime promise to him and ourselves to *never* end a day without dealing with any issue that had come between us. We believe that decision is one of the secrets of our long-term, exceedingly happy marriage.

How can we deal with the conflicts that divide us? The simple answer is to forgive and confess our own less-than-holy responses. A more holistic answer includes working through the issues that hurt and divide and finding biblical ways to solve them.

Overcoming temptation. Temptation has been the devil's major ploy from the beginning. Satan attempts to entrap us in any kind of sin he can.

Jesus experienced forty days of intense temptation by Satan himself. The enemy challenged his identity, tempted him to use his divine power rather than depend on his Father, and offered him the whole world (without the cross) if Jesus would only fall down and worship him (Matthew 4:1-11).

Jesus demonstrates *how* to defeat the temptations of the enemy. He overcame each of them by fasting and prayer and by quoting appropriate truth from Scripture *verbatim*. Each verse was carefully chosen to directly contradict the lie being proffered. Jesus ended the attack of the enemy by commanding him to leave. He spoke aloud one brief, authoritative word: "Away from me, Satan." And the devil left him (Matthew 4:10-11).

Attacks from without. If Satan can neutralize us as Christians, bringing us down through attacks from within, we become minimal threats to his kingdom and low maintenance projects. He is very happy to keep us as we are.[19]

However, if we overcome the attacks from within and partner with Jesus to advance his kingdom, we may experience a different kind of enemy assault coming from the *outside*, through harassment, persecution and suffering. This kind of attack comes not because we are doing something wrong but because we are doing something right.[20]

Overcoming the enemy's harassments and "flaming arrows." Paul experienced continual attacks from the enemy, including a "thorn in the flesh," which God chose not to remove (2 Corinthians 12:7-10). Satan opposed Paul's pastoral visits to Thessalonica. "We wanted to come to you . . . again and again—but Satan stopped us" (1 Thessalonians 2:18). Paul does not reveal how he knew that his difficulties were the direct assaults of the devil, but he prayed to God when they arose rather than addressing the enemy. Sensing Satan's desire to destroy this young church, he wrote these encouraging words for them and for us: "The Lord is faithful, and he will strengthen you and protect you from the evil one" (2 Thessalonians 3:3).

Harassments and fiery darts can come in all shapes and sizes: sudden, unexplainable, severe pain; doubts, fears or temptations that seem to come out of nowhere; or a rash of accidents, mishaps or breakdowns. We know of a group translating the Bible into an indigenous language in Brazil whose photocopying machine would reproduce *any* document except biblical texts about the devil and his lies. They had to pray against this demonic assault.

How can we resist and overcome these kinds of attacks? First Peter 5:5-11 provides helpful guidelines:

"Humble yourselves . . . under God's mighty hand" (v. 6). This could include worshiping, affirming our trust in him, confessing any known sin, forgiving those who have hurt us and putting on God's armor.

"Cast all your anxiety on him because he cares for you" (v. 7). This could include crying out to God about the harassment, asking for discernment about where it's coming from and asking for wisdom about how to deal with it, receiving any Scripture God might give.

"Your enemy . . . prowls around like a roaring lion looking for someone to devour" (v. 8). We are to "resist him, standing firm in the faith" (v. 9). We can do this by praying Scripture passages like 1 John 3:8, Isaiah 54:17, Psalm 35:1-10 and Psalm 144:5-8. We can also bind the enemy (Matthew 12:29) and command him to leave as Jesus did (Matthew 4:10).

Tom White suggests we pray a prayer like this:

Satan, I resist you in the authority of Jesus Christ. I declare your works in my life destroyed. Jesus triumphed over you in the wilderness, on the cross, and in the grave. His resurrection has sealed your fate. I triumph over you now in the strength of His name. I rebuke your efforts to oppress, afflict or deceive me. I remove from you the right to rob me of the joy and fruit of my salvation. Through the power of the blood of Calvary, I command all powers of darkness assigned to or sent to me to leave. Go where Jesus Christ orders you to go.[21]

Overcoming suffering and persecution. During the early days of our ministry in Bogotá, one of the Marxist factions involved in the National University became inflamed with anger and disdain toward all the Christian students on campus. They ridiculed our evangelistic outreaches and Bible studies, and accused us of having a nonscientific (read: non-Marxist) worldview. One day their hostility boiled over into raging persecution. They snatched some of the students' Bibles, publicly burned them and then drove the believers off campus in a hail of stones.

Some of these students came to our student center just across the street from campus. We bathed their wounds, worshiped together and studied Acts 4:23-31. Tears ran down our cheeks as we heard them pray the prayer of the early church: "Now, Lord, consider their threats and enable your servants to speak your word with great boldness" (v. 29).

The very next day these Christian students returned to campus and went from one classroom to another. Their message:

> Yesterday you Marxists, who speak continually about justice, were totally unjust to us. We too are students and have a right to be here. We are not coming today to express anger. We want you to know that we forgive you because Jesus has forgiven us and put his love in our hearts for you. We proclaim him.

Suffering is an integral part of our Christian lives. We grow in Christ's image as we share in his suffering. It is also a privilege given to us by God: "It has been granted to you on behalf of Christ not only to believe in him, but also to suffer for him" (Philippians 1:29).

Although Christian groups in North America may not be persecuted physically, many experience the pain and privilege of opposition. Alec Hill, president of InterVarsity Christian Fellowship/USA, wrote in early 2012:

> Currently, the right of Christian groups to conduct their fellowship according to historic Christian doctrine is being challenged, to varying degrees at 41 different universities. We rejoice that at many of these schools, students and administrators have found common ground. And where that has not happened, InterVarsity student leaders and staff are not abandoning their beliefs.[22]

These experiences should not surprise us. Jesus said, "If the world hates you, keep in mind that it hated me first" (John 15:18). "If they persecuted me, they will persecute you also" (John 15:20). "They will do such things because they have not known the Father or me" (John 16:3). "All this I have told you so that you will not fall away" (John 16:1). "Peace I leave with you; my peace I give you. . . . Do not let your hearts be troubled and do not be afraid" (John 14:27). "In this world you will have trouble. But take heart! I have overcome the world" (John 16:33).

ADVANCING THE KINGDOM, THE TRUE GOAL OF SPIRITUAL WARFARE

Ever since the Fall, God has been on a mission to undo its effects through the life, death and resurrection of his Son. He desires to rescue people of every race, tribe, culture and nation from the grip of an enemy who connives to hold them in spiritual darkness and death.

We want to complete our exploration of spiritual warfare by looking at four valuable spiritual weapons that can help us partner with Jesus as he advances God's kingdom in the world.

The power of worship. "As they began to sing and praise, the LORD set ambushes against the men . . . who were invading Judah, and they were defeated" (2 Chronicles 20:22). King Jehoshaphat learned that when we focus on the Lord and proclaim his glory, power and holiness, he defeats the enemy. Actually, "no one can do warfare who is not first a worshiper of God."[23]

After the blatant attack on T. V. Thomas, we greatly intensified our efforts in prayer until we learned of an even better way to go forward. We heard the amazing story of Jenny Mayhew, an intercessor who prays for nations. Her preferred method of intercession is contemplative worship, including recorded song, praying Scripture passages of praise and heartfelt adoration.

One day, knowing that Afghanistan was experiencing a severe three-year drought, Jenny felt led to go there, find a place to stay and worship God day and night for seven days, trusting him for rain. She took a friend to worship with her and to spell her off when she rested. When they finished, it rained for twenty-four hours straight. Students at Bethany College in Minneapolis were so inspired by Jenny's story they developed an ongoing worship ministry.

As prayer leaders for Urbana 03, Mary Anne and Lisa Laird asked permission to have a team from Bethany lead an ongoing worship room in Assembly Hall throughout the whole convention.

Day after day they observed amazing "coincidences." It was the mildest winter anyone could remember. For the first time on record none of the crisis counselors had to get out of bed at night to deal with emergencies. Few delegates were sick and only one had to be hospitalized. It was an Urbana with less spiritual attack than the intercessors had ever experienced.

On the last evening a supervisor suggested they close the worship room early since the convention ended at midnight. After the order was given, Mary Anne received twelve urgent phone calls informing her of things that were going wrong, including a glitch in the usually flawless Communion service. Lisa rushed to the worship room to ask them to continue, but they already knew and had reinitiated worship. As they did so, the problems began to ease. God seemed to want everyone to know that as we worshiped him, he had taken care of everything else.

Tom White, who has faced much spiritual warfare, feels worship is the best way to overcome it.

> Praise is an act of faith that affirms the character and redemptive power of God in all circumstances. If God truly dwells in the praises of his people, the regular practice of praise must be built into the lifestyle of the spiritual warrior. I used to feel weighed down by the burden of spiritual battles, but then I learned a secret. God waits for us to praise Him so he can pour out His strength in us. Praise releases divine power.[24]

The power of prayer. "Prayer isn't so much another weapon on the list of our weaponry," comments Dick Eastman, "as it is the actual battle itself."[25]

Corporate, unified intercession intensified by fasting is another powerful way of waging offensive spiritual warfare. Our best prayer book and guide to praying God's will is the Bible itself. When interceding for a critical event the two of us have often found it helpful to set aside a whole day for prayer and fasting while praying through an entire epistle (like Ephesians or Colossians) for the people we'll be teaching. We read one verse at a time and turn it into praise to God or a prayer for ourselves or others.

Jason Gaboury tells us that the outreach events of InterVarsity in the New York/New Jersey region have been much more fruitful since they decided to have intercession teams praying behind the scenes, interceding for non-Christians and standing against enemy attacks.

One evening in a commuter school, an evangelistic meeting was about to begin. Suddenly, with no warning, campus security came in and demanded that the room be cleared. Jason's wife, Sophia, texted the intercessors upstairs and asked them to pray (1) that the students would stick around, (2) for a quick resolution and (3) for God to soften hearts to the gospel.

The students didn't leave, the resolution to the security problem was quick, and in the process InterVarsity students had the opportunity to interact with the newcomers. Throughout the rest of the night Sophia would text the intercessors with information about what was happening below, like, "gospel being summarized . . . pray for clarity and conviction." The intercessors would pray and text back images, words or Scripture they sensed God was giving them, like, "We're praying for courage to respond to Jesus." At the end of the evening one of the intercessors asked Sophia how many people had responded to the invitation to follow Jesus. Sophia told her "eighteen." She then showed Sophia the number of students that they had felt God inviting them to pray for. The numbers were the same.[26]

Prayer and bold outreach were working hand in hand to advance the kingdom on that campus.

The power of the proclamation of the Word. The role of Scripture has been critical in our own lives and in the growth of evangelical student movements everywhere. God's truth is a powerful two-edged sword that penetrates hearts, uproots the lies of the enemy and plants new seeds of life and transformation.

Years ago a young seeker came to live with us during the summer vacation. Each night Jack and our new friend studied a few verses from the book of James. When they came to James 1:17-18 the young man was riveted by these words: "Every good and perfect gift is from above, coming down from the Father of the heavenly lights, who does not change like shifting shadows. He chose to give us birth through the word of truth."

"Is that really true," he queried, "that God never changes? All my life I have been searching for something solid and unchangeable, on which I could build my life."

That night "the word of truth" brought him new birth and transformed his life. He became a lover of Scripture and an effective Bible teacher to this day.

The power of costly love and courageous witness. The advance of the kingdom doesn't proceed exclusively through verbal communication. Genuine Christians have to *live* the gospel before they can explain it in words. Unconditional, loving service is costly but redemptive.

The Peruvian IFES movement prayed for humble ways to lovingly serve their classmates. Most of the students came from poor families, and many of their non-Christian friends saw Marxism as the best road to justice. Jesus had no place in their hearts.

Several of the Christian students already cooked simple lunches for those who had no money, but what else could they do? As they looked around for a place to serve, their eyes fell on the filthy campus bathrooms. If they worked together they could clean places that would serve every single student. Without a word they silently began.

The non-Christians noticed their ongoing faithful cleaning service, but said nothing. Over time, this silent testimony opened small doors in hearts. Weeks later, ears were also opened and willing to listen as Christian students went from classroom to classroom courageously sharing their faith in Jesus. They invited their classmates to study Scripture and to meet the only One who can transform lives.

PUTTING IT ALL TOGETHER

What do all these principles of spiritual warfare and mission look like in real life?

Right after their honeymoon, Scott and Connie Anderson felt called to begin an InterVarsity chapter at a college originally founded to train missionaries. What a contrast they encountered! There was no Christian presence on campus, professors scheduled exams on Easter Sunday, and a coven of witches held séances in the dorms and rituals in the campus amphitheater.

If you were the Andersons, how would you have approached such a situation? They tell us in their own words.

> We were young in experience, bold in prayer and deeply in love with Jesus. We felt called to this campus and believed that the walls of opposition would crumble in response to prayer and worship of the One True God.
>
> Our supervisor called us saying that he sensed a strong evil spirit coming against us. We enlisted local believers to intercede, prayer walked the campus, weighed the guidance we received by the Scripture, and continued to follow Jesus and make him known.
>
> The results? Forty students signed up for the first Bible studies. Student leadership, conversions, Greek outreach, ministry to migrant workers and summer missions all blossomed. The witches dwindled and we started holding Easter services in the amphitheater. The darkest dorm became the home of multiple Bible studies and prayer meetings. In four years nearly 10% of the campus became involved in the fellowship. Eight InterVarsity staff and numerous missionaries came out of that community. Twenty years later, the fellowship is still going strong.
>
> A barren field became a fruitful garden.
>
> To be sure, every time we took a leap forward in ministry we would get significant opposition. But we clung to the promise we felt we had received, that the walls of darkness, opposition, and idolatry would fall in response to believing, faithful prayer.[27]

Questions for Personal Reflection or Group Discussion

1. As you read this booklet and consider the Scripture passages and stories, how have they changed or expanded your understanding of spiritual warfare?

2. In what ways have you experienced spiritual warfare and how might you be better prepared to deal with it now?

3. Tom White says, "The greatest preparation for spiritual warfare is pre-occupation with the person of Jesus and an unshakable faith in his triumph over evil."[28] How would you compare and contrast the power of Satan and the power of Jesus? How central and real is Jesus to you?

4. Victory over the enemy begins with the name of Jesus on our lips but is not complete until the nature of Jesus is reflected in our lives. Evaluate the quality of your devotional life, your practice of worship and prayer and your growth in Christlikeness. What do you discover?

5. In what ways are you experiencing enemy attacks from *within:*

    •   Through Satan's lies about your identity or worth? (How could you confront them?)

    •   Through habitual sin or powerful temptations you haven't been able to overcome? (How does Jesus' example help you deal with these?)

    •   Through relationships that need forgiveness and reconciliation?

    •   You may want to share some of these areas with your small group and pray for each other.

6. God's chief strategies and weapons for overcoming the enemy include:

    •   knowing Jesus as Savior and Lord

    •   being filled with the Spirit and living a holy life

    •   worshiping God and interceding with others

    •   lovingly proclaiming the gospel in word, deed and testimony

    How would you evaluate your own life and that of your community in terms of advancing God's kingdom in these ways? What are you doing well and where could you improve?

7. If you are experiencing the enemy's harassment or persecution as you seek to make Christ known, be encouraged by these words of the apostle Paul: "Thanks be to God, who always leads us as captives in Christ's triumphal procession and uses us to spread the aroma of the knowledge of him everywhere" (2 Corinthians 2:14).

→   →   →

SUGGESTED READING

Anderson, Neil, and Rich Miller. *Steps to Freedom*. La Habra, Calif.: Freedom in Christ, 1997.

Arnold, Clinton E. *Three Crucial Questions About Spiritual Warfare*. Grand Rapids: Baker, 1997.

MacNutt, Francis. *Deliverance from Evil Spirits: A Practical Manual*. Grand Rapids: Chosen Books, 1995.

White, Thomas B. *The Believer's Guide to Spiritual Warfare*. Ann Arbor, Mich.: Servant, 2011.

NOTES

[1]Lisa Laird, InterVarsity Campus Ministry Director in Saskatchewan, personal correspondence with the authors, January 19, 2012.

[2]International Fellowship of Evangelical Students, the umbrella organization of which InterVarsity is a member together with UCU of Colombia, AGEUP of Peru and scores of other national student movements.

[3]Derek Prince, *Spiritual Warfare* (New Kensington, Penn.: Whitakerhouse, 1987), p. 35.

[4]C. S. Lewis, *Screwtape Letters* (San Francisco: HarperCollins, 1942), p. ix.

[5]Clinton E. Arnold, *Three Crucial Questions About Spiritual Warfare* (Grand Rapids: Baker, 1997), p. 34.

[6]Jason Gaboury, email to the authors, January 19, 2012.

[7]P. E. Hughes, "Fall," in *New Bible Dictionary*, ed. I. Howard Marshall et al., 3rd ed. (Downers Grove, Ill.: InterVarsity Press, 1996), p. 360.

[8]Mary Ellen Conners, "Spiritual Warfare 101," in *Prayer and Intercession Training Manual*, ed. Mary Anne Voelkel and Judith Allen Shelly (Madison, Wis.: InterVarsity Christian Fellowship, 2008), p. 135.

[9]Charles Kraft, *I Give You Authority* (Grand Rapids: Chosen, 1997), p. 67.

[10]Mary Anne remembers Mike Flynn sharing this experience in three conferences she attended.

[11]In the New Testament the Greek text never uses the literal expression "demon possessed." Rather, the term *demonized* is a transliteration of the Greek word *daimonizomai*, which can give the impression of being either heavily "influenced" by a demon or having a demon actually resident within the individual, but not *possessed* in the sense of the evil spirit completely controlling the very center of an individual's personality.

[12]Thomas B. White, *The Believer's Guide to Spiritual Warfare* (Ann Arbor, Mich.: Servant, 2011), p. 64.

[13]Ibid., p. 44.

[14]Arnold, *Three Crucial Questions About Spiritual Warfare*, pp. 108, 124.

[15]White, *Believer's Guide to Spiritual Warfare*, p. 68.

[16]Neil T. Anderson and Rich Miller, *Steps to Freedom in Christ for Young Adults* (La Habra, Calif.: Freedom in Christ, 1997).

[17]Jason Gaboury, email to prayer partners, January 26, 2012.

[18]White, *Believer's Guide to Spiritual Warfare*, p. 100.

[19]Ibid., p. 60.

[20]Ibid., p. 113.

[21]Ibid., p. 164.

[22]Alec Hill. "Pray for Student Ministry at Vanderbilt," an InterVarsity prayer letter sent by email, February 8, 2012.

[23]Franciso Frangipane, *Army of Worshipers*. Adapted from Franciso Frangipane, *The Three Battlegrounds* (Cedar Rapids, Iowa: Arrow, 1989).

[24]White, *Believer's Guide to Spiritual Warfare*, p. 218.

[25]Dick Eastman, *Love on Its Knees* (Old Tappan, N.J.: Chosen, 1989), p. 65.

[26]Jason Gaboury, personal email. Sophia is an area director of InterVarsity Christian Fellowship.

[27]Scott and Connie Anderson, email to the authors, February 3, 2012.

[28]White, *Believer's Guide to Spiritual Warfare*, p. 74.

About Urbana

Since InterVarsity Christian Fellowship/USA and Inter-Varsity Canada's first Student Missions Conference in 1946, Urbana has influenced more than 250,000 people to devote their lives to God's global mission. Urbana's mission is to compel this generation to give their whole lives for God's global mission. Participants are challenged by missions leaders, are able to speak with hundreds of missions organizations, get to attend an amazing selection of seminars and tracks, and study the Bible inductively with other students listening for God's call on their lives. For more information, visit www.urbana.org.

Urbana Onward

God calls us to go into the world as his representatives. But we need not travel alone. Urbana Onward provides companions for the lifelong journey into missional living. This series offers concise resources for grappling with challenging issues. Trusted authors provide biblical and practical insights for following God's call in creative and courageous ways. Discover a bigger picture of God's global mission as he leads you onward.

Pursuing God's Call by Tom Lin, 978-0-8308-3459-4

Partnering with the Global Church by Nikki A. Toyama-Szeto and Femi B. Adeleye, 978-0-8308-3460-0

The Mission of Worship by Sandra Van Opstal, 978-0-8308-3462-4

Your Mind's Mission by Greg Jao, 978-0-8308-3461-7

Deepening the Soul for Justice by Bethany H. Hoang, 978-0-8308-3463-1

Spiritual Warfare in Mission by Mary Anne and Jack Voelkel, 978-0-8308-3464-8